OXFORDSHIRE
CUSTOMS, SPORTS
& TRADITIONS

MARILYN YURDAN

T0333147

The History Press

In the mid-1980s, the then Lord Mayor, Dr Frank Garside, revived 'Riding the Franchise', which consists of a tour of the town boundaries. The most spectacular aspect of this is the sight of the Lord Mayor, together with the Vice-Chancellor, inspecting the medieval wall in New College. They do this in accordance with the terms by which William of Wykeham, the college founder, was allowed to purchase the site; these stipulated that the fortifications were to be kept in good repair. So conscientiously has this been done by the college that this stretch of wall, together with another in Deadman's Walk south of Merton College, are the only sections of the wall to survive. This photograph shows the 1996 Lord Mayor's inspection, which now takes place every three years.

First published 2011
Reprinted 2020

The History Press
97 St George's Place, Cheltenham,
Gloucestershire, GL50 3QB
www.thehistorypress.co.uk

British Library Cataloguing in Publication Data.
A catalogue record for this book is available from the British Library.

ISBN 978 0 7524 5743 7
Typesetting and origination by The History Press
Printed in Great Britain by TJ International Ltd, Padstow, Cornwall.

CONTENTS

ACKNOWLEDGEMENTS

Many thanks to John Brown, Chris McDowell and Newsquest Oxfordshire Picture Library, which supplied the majority of the photographs in this book.

The present Chancellor of the University of Oxford, the Rt Hon. Chris Patten, is shown entering the Sheldonian Theatre with the Public Orator, Dr Jasper Griffin, immediately after his installation on 25 June 2003. The office of Chancellor dates back to about 1224 and early holders were the Bishops of Lincoln, in whose huge diocese Oxford was then situated. Later Chancellors were resident members of the University and today they are elected from suitable nominees by members of Congregation (anyone who holds an Oxford degree) who have to come to Oxford and vote in person. It is an ideal opportunity to spot celebrities among the queues waiting to register their votes.

INTRODUCTION

Due to the fact that Oxfordshire is an ancient and largely rural county, it has retained some of the traditions and customs which have been discarded in more industrialised parts of the country. Some activities are part of nationwide celebrations, but others are unusual and some even unique to Oxfordshire. The city of Oxford itself retains more quirky traditions than most other county towns, largely thanks to the presence of the University.

Some of Oxfordshire's historical events are genuine survivors and date back centuries, notably the sounding of the curfew at Wallingford and the St John the Baptist Day sermon given from the outdoor pulpit at Magdalen College. Some, like Beating the Bounds at Woodstock, the inspection of the section of the city wall in New College and Riding the Franchise at Oxford died out but have been reintroduced in the nineteenth and twentieth centuries. Others, however, are unashamedly modern but have caught the popular imagination and have therefore become regular happenings. A leading example is the Great Shirt Race at Bampton, which claims to have originated in King Ethelred the Shirtless's frantic search for something to wear but dates only from the last century.

The coronation of the present Queen in June 1953 has been given a chapter to itself. A coronation is one of the most historic occasions that anyone will witness in their lifetime and this one was particularly impressive. Not only did it take place shortly after the end of wartime austerity, but it was noteworthy as being the first (and of course to date the only) coronation to have been televised. For thousands of people it was the first television which they had seen and those households that could afford to do so bought a television set specially and invited privileged friends and neighbours round to watch.

Oxford's May Morning celebrations – when the choir of Magdalen College welcome in the spring from the top of its tower, Morris dancers perform at various venues in the city and dozens of young people take out punts on the river – are known worldwide. At one time most towns and villages erected a maypole and chose a May Queen (and sometimes a King), and the tradition is carried on in several places to this day.

The county is one of the leading areas for Morris dancing and has been since at least Tudor times (and probably back into the Middle Ages). Although Headington is credited with being the village which brought about the revival of this type of dancing, it is quite clear that in several places it never died out. Today most of the market towns and several villages have at least one 'side' or troupe, notably Bampton and Abingdon.

Less common are the mummers' plays, most of which are performed over the festive season, usually in public houses or their car parks. The players are frequently also Morris dancers. The principal villages which carry on the tradition are Headington, Blewbury and Sunningwell and while communities have their own versions of the plays, there are characters in them which are common to mumming plays all over the country. The two overlaying themes of the performances are as old as man himself: the struggle between good and evil and that of death being followed by rebirth.

The last two decades have seen a profusion of new carnivals, shows, exhibitions, fun days, processions, open days, craft and country fairs of all kinds, many of which are set to become traditions in their own right. Leading examples are the Cornbury and Towersey festivals and Fairport's Cropredy Convention. Besides giving pleasure to the whole family, such events raise huge amounts of money for local and national charities. It is good to find, too, that most of the old fairs and markets, the majority of which date back to medieval times, are still very much a going concern. Small funfairs spring up in parks and on village greens during the spring and summer but the principal season for fairs is between mid-September and early October, and are descendents of the ancient hiring fairs which took place around Michaelmas, the 29th September.

The Oxfordshire sports which spring immediately to mind are rowing and rugby, particularly when they are played against Cambridge in the University Boat Race on the Thames in London and at Twickenham respectively. Individual colleges take to the river for the Torpid rowing races in February and the more famous Eights in May. There is an increasing number of waterside activities, from the world-renowned Henley Regatta to the increasingly popular dragon-boat racing. Less common are Pooh Sticks and Aunt Sally, which are very much Oxfordshire activities.

Two more types of activity which might loosely be termed games (and which became popular in the University but died out towards the end of the twentieth century) were hoaxes and practical jokes. At worst these could be a form of vandalism, at best they involved some very skilful acting and hours of patient preparation.

The red-letter days which mark the passing of an Oxfordshire Year, many of which are related to religious festivals, are not of course all confined to the county but every community celebrates in its own individual way. Oxford's sizeable Welsh community marks St David's Day on 1st March with concerts given by its male voice choirs, and its Irish dancers and ceilidh performers honour St Patrick on 17th March. By contrast, tributes to St Andrew and Rabbie Burns take place largely behind closed doors, and until very recently St George was seldom mentioned.

As elsewhere, we celebrate national high days and holidays like Christmas, Easter and Guy Fawkes Night with one or two quirky additions of our own, many of which are related to the University.

There are three terms, Michaelmas, Hilary and Trinity, each full term lasting eight weeks, and the academic year differs from the calendar one in that it starts in October with Michaelmas Term and finishes with the Long Vacation which extends over the summer months.

Marilyn Yurdan, 2011

1

HISTORICAL EVENTS

In April 1974, the 418-year-old Borough of Abingdon ceased to exist. Its disappearance
was marked by a three-day event which included a banquet, a Freedom ceremony, the
unveiling of a foundation stone, bun-throwing and a civic service. At the same time, the
'new' Abingdon was welcomed as the focal point of the recently-created local authority, the
Vale of White Horse. This reorganisation meant that the oldest continually inhabited town
in Britain and former county town of Berkshire was now in Oxfordshire. This photograph
captured the moment when, says the *Oxford Times*, 'to the delight of the spectators and the
dismay of the organisers and the Mayor, the silk balloon holding little balloons collapsed on
top of the guests.'

The construction of a chopping block measuring 25ft by 3ft was celebrated at Magdalen College in 1981. The wood was taken from a 150-year-old elm which was cut down in the college grounds 100 years ago. For the celebrations past and present kitchen staff gathered on the college saint's day, 22nd July. *Chef de cuisine* Roger Webster, with former chefs Ken Butler and Bill Jarvis, composed an eight-verse 'Ode to the Kitchen Block' in its honour.

A village event of very long standing, in which the whole village is involved, is the Lamb Ale feast at Kirtlington. This photograph from June 1965 shows members of the Lamb Ale committee having lunch before watching the Morris dancing, which forms a traditional part of the celebrations. Old records describe how the village girls would chase a lamb through the streets with their thumbs tied behind their backs, the one who caught it being called 'the Lady of the Lamb'.

Henley women clog dancers performing at Kirtlington Lamb Ale in June 1983. The tradition of the Lady survives, as does the Morris dancing. In 1983 dancers from fourteen sides took part in the weekend, which started with a ceilidh and continued with a 'Folkie' tea-party, a sing-song and a procession through the village, and ended with a church service. In former days, festivities lasted a week and also included a cricket match between villagers and a team from Merton College.

Mr Frederick Warmington being given his chain of office at the Rose and Crown in August 1958. The 'Election of the Mock Mayor of Old Woodstock' dates back at least to 1786. The Mayor, together with his Corporation, is elected with all due ceremony – and then promptly tossed into the River Glyme which separates Old and New Woodstock. On this occasion, several of the new Mayor's fellow councillors were thrown in too, to the cry of 'He wants some company!' The origins of this election lie in the fact that because, until 1866, the Borough of Woodstock was separate from Old Woodstock, which formed part of the parish and royal manor of Wootton, residents decided to hold their own elections. The voting takes place every August and is accompanied by a fête and followed by live music in the evening.

This is the wooden mace used every year during the election of the Mock Mayor of Old Woodstock. It was put on show at the Town Hall in March 1959 as part of a display of Woodstock's treasures. Holding it aloft is Councillor D. Donovan and admiring the mace are Town Clerk Victor Tolley, Miss F. Grierson and Miss S. Haynes.

This photograph of the official Mayor of Woodstock, Councillor Mrs M.E. Bowley, and the Woodstock Borough Council was taken in May 1962. Also in the picture are the Duke of Marlborough (middle row, far left) and Councillor Bowley's daughter Catherine, who acted as her mother's Mayoress during her year in office. At this date the future of the town's status as a borough was in the balance and all the members of the Council were aware that this was a historic moment. The town is now represented by a Town Council.

In this photograph, taken in July 1962, local farmers had gathered to bid for the hay crop in meadows at Yarnton. By this date only three of the medieval meadows remained. The land belonged to five owners and the conditions under which the mowing rights could be sold had little changed in the course of 500 years. The fields had names such as Gilbert, William of Bladon, Bolton, Parry and Rothe (which are thought to be those of long-dead tenants).

The first recorded occasion when buns were thrown at Abingdon was to mark the coronation of George III although it could well have occurred earlier than this. Since then, on days of national importance, thousands of specially designed buns have been thrown from the flat part of the roof of the Shire down into the surrounding Market Place. In November 1986, when this photograph was taken, the occasion was the wedding of Prince Andrew and Sarah Ferguson. More recent ones included the Queen's Diamond Jubilee and the Millennium. The most recent bun-throwing was for the Queen's Golden Jubilee in 2002. A collection of buns, one from each 'throwing', is kept in Abingdon Museum, the oldest dating from Queen Victoria's Golden Jubilee in 1887. There will be a 'throwing' to mark the royal wedding in April 2011.

Above: One of the privileges of being a Freeman of Abingdon is having the right to walk one's sheep over the town bridge. Shown with a couple of token sheep in January 2001 are a crowd which includes Abingdon's Town Crier, its Mayor, Councillor Lesley Legge, and farmer Gervase Duffield. It was hoped that the custom could be revived to mark the Millennium, but this did not materialise, partly because of concerns for the animals' welfare.

Right: According to another ancient custom, the annual rent paid by the Mayor of Wallingford on behalf of the town for the lease of Wallingford castle and grounds is a tree. In October 1980 it was a cherry tree, which the Mayor, Mr Alec Goode, is shown planting in the garden of the castle's owner, Sir John Hedges. The castle was started by its Norman builders in 1067, only a year after the Conquest.

Wallingford was one of King Alfred's fortified burghs and is still proud of its heritage, which included the privilege of being allowed an extra hour after the general curfew, 9 p.m. instead of 8 p.m., as a mark of the townspeople's co-operation with their Norman overlords. The bell still rings out just before 9 p.m. every evening. In June 1995 another old custom was revived when the Town Clerk, Bernard Picken, called on the Mayor, the Revd Ian Beckwith, to escort him to the Town Hall (accompanied by the mace-bearer, councillors and aldermen).

Left: In May 1981, the Mayor of Wallingford, Mr Bill Revel, took the salute at a march-past in the Market Place during the Mayor's church service and parade. Taking part were representatives from nearby RAF Benson and members of the town's Red Cross, the Girls' Venture Unit, the Scouts and Sea Scouts, Guides and Brownies. The Mayor is pictured setting off for the annual service at St Mary's church, followed by the civic reception at the Town Hall.

Below: In July 1996 the peace was shattered in the gardens surrounding Wallingford Castle when members of the Sealed Knot Society re-enacted the noisy and violent siege by Parliamentarian troops in 1646. No stranger to siege warfare, this Royalist stronghold managed to withstand their onslaught for sixty-five days, only to be demolished in 1652 after the Civil War was over. These twentieth-century pike men played a very prominent role, and the struggle appeared to be dangerously realistic.

There was further activity from the Sealed Knot Society re-enacting the Civil War in Wallingford in July 1996, when Roundhead horsemen rode through the Market Place on their heavy horses. They were marking the surrender, by General Thomas Blagge, of the castle – which was the last one to remain loyal to Charles I – to General Fairfax in July 1646. Blagge had threatened to set fire to the town if Parliament attacked the castle, but a mutiny in the garrison brought forward its capitulation by two days.

The second part of the twentieth century saw a revival of some customs which had been allowed to lapse. In Oxford some parish boundaries are still beaten on Ascension Day, but the time of year varies elsewhere in the county. In March 1974 the Mayor of Banbury, Councillor Don Fraser, took part in a nineteenth-century custom which had died out more than twenty years previously. This was Beating the Bounds, and involved wellington boots and wooden mallets on loan from Banbury museum. These were first used in 1889, for driving in a number of stakes which marked the town boundaries. The revival was to mark the fact that the Town Council would cease to exist on 1st April 1974.

These four schoolgirls, Ann Gardner, Anne Vine, Jean Bonham and Jean Woodfield, wore seventeenth-century costume in order to publicise Cropredy Village Fair in June 1965. The period costume was a reference to the Battle of Cropredy Bridge, which took place in 1644 during the Civil War. The three celebrities who performed the Fair's opening ceremony were John Betjeman, Government Minister Richard Crossman (who lived in the village), and fellow MP Neil Marten.

The first Wychwood Forest Fairs were organised towards the end of the eighteenth century in a bid to offer an alternative to other drunken and disorderly local fairs. They were held under the auspices of the Churchill family of nearby Blenheim Palace and became something of a social event, attracting thousands of visitors. However, the fair was suppressed by the Duke of Marlborough in 1856 due to alleged 'drunkenness and debauchery'. This revived Wychwood Forest Fair, held at Charlbury in October 1972, was opened by the Duchess of Marlborough, who is shown here chatting to entrants in the fancy-dress competition.

Another town Mayor, Councillor John Banbury, also took part in a revived Beating of the Bounds ceremony in March 1974. This was at Woodstock and was only the fourth time that the ceremony had been performed in the previous 112 years. The route taken was that defined by the Charter granted by Queen Victoria in 1886. Obstacles to be surmounted included the 10ft wall of Blenheim Palace, and the River Glyme, which Councillor Banbury is shown crossing in a punt.

As part of the ceremony of Beating of the Bounds at Woodstock in 1974, Mr Banbury was bumped against a boundary mark. Holding him carefully but none too gently are Town Clerk Martin Sawyer and Councillor Glyn Williams. The man-handling recalls the days when choirboys as well as markers were beaten in order to impress on them where the boundaries were.

In October 1974, the Beating of the Bounds ceremony was revived at Steventon for the first time in the twentieth century. This was organised by the village's Amenity Group to stimulate an interest in local history. Seventeen beaters toured the parish's 9.5 mile boundary, searching for ancient boundary stones; they found two, which they duly beat. The vicar, Dr A.M.G. Stephenson, is shown seeing the beaters off as they leave the church.

In June 1984 this part of the recently-revived ceremony of Riding the Franchise (or boundaries) of the City of Oxford was accompanied by a group of musicians playing ancient instruments loaned by the University's Faculty of Music, and wearing costumes lent by the Playhouse. Members of the band, some of whom were students, specialised in music from the thirteenth to the seventeenth century and went under the ancient name of the Oxford City Waits. Historically, waits were singers and musicians who played on civic occasions and were to be found in most medieval towns and cities.

These Northmoor maidens (Peta Beck, Michelle Harris, Lucy Reeves and Donna and Lisa Hutt), posing with their baskets of apples, were taking part in the Apple Fair, which had been revived for the third year running in September 1976. With them is the vicar, the Reverend Michael Farthing, astride Shandy, the bay pony. The tradition, which had lapsed for 152 years, was rediscovered when a parishioner came across a reference to it in a history of the village. The object was to throw apples into a 'wishing bower' in order to make wishes come true.

Abingdon has a long and proud tradition of welcoming visitors dating back to its time as a medieval abbey; members of the royal family once spent Christmas or Easter there. In July 1979, historical tours of Abingdon were introduced by the Abingdon Archaeological and Historical Society, whose members arranged guided tours showing summer visitors something of the town's varied history. Not surprisingly, these turned out to be very popular, especially with local people.

For centuries the end of a war has been an occasion for thanksgiving and celebration. In June 1983, glasses were raised at the Falkland Arms at Great Tew as part of celebrations to mark the first anniversary of victory in the Falklands conflict. Pictured in the forefront is former paratrooper Bob Spencer, who fought in the battle to relieve Fort Stanley and was then working as a lifeguard at Chipping Norton swimming pool. Both the islands and the pub were named after the family who owned the Great Tew estate in the seventeenth century.

Each of the Oxford colleges has an official visitor, a person of national importance who attends on important occasions. On 25th May 1948, when the degree of Doctor of Civil Law was conferred on the present Queen, while she was still Princess Elizabeth, she took the opportunity of going to Oriel College, where she is the visitor. In Front Quad she was introduced to OC, the Oriel Tortoise, which upstaged the Provost and Fellows by marching up to the royal feet. The back page of *The Times* carried a feature on this high-profile encounter.

2

THE 1953 CORONATION

The Lord Mayor and Mayoress of Oxford, Councillor A.B. and Mrs Brown, cut this very ornate cake, given by Councillor J.R.S. Duke, at the street party organised for the children of St John Street and Beaumont Buildings to celebrate the coronation of Queen Elizabeth II. Afterwards, each of the sixty children was given a present. In an article written in 1977 for the Silver Jubilee, the *Oxford Mail* remarked that 'Oxford was hooked on TV and in those days that meant drawn curtains ... It might have been a day of national mourning.'

Activities in the county's villages were much livelier. This photograph, taken in June 1953, shows the children of Adderbury posing in fancy dress on the village green shortly before the coronation party. In addition to the usual pirates and cowboys, some of the children are dressed in costumes representing various countries of the Commonwealth.

These are some of the children who took part in the fancy-dress competition during the coronation celebrations at Benson. It's a pity that we have no record of what it is that is capturing the attention of the people in the photograph.

At Bloxham, coronation celebrations took the form of a travelling carnival, which linked the events which were going on at various points throughout the village. This group is made up exclusively of adults who are dressed up to the nines, whereas the younger generation, coming along behind in a cart, are wearing their everyday clothes.

Charlbury's coronation activities also included a carnival made up of children and adults who paraded through the main streets. In this photograph they are shown coming along Sheep Street in the centre of the town.

Opposite below: Cotswold Crescent in Chipping Norton organised its own coronation festivities and invited the town's Mayor and Mayoress. They came along and posed for the camera, surrounded by local children in fancy dress which included several queens, a Britannia and even an Invisible Man (front, centre).

At Chipping Norton the Town Mayor and Mayoress pose on the steps of the Town Hall for this commemorative photograph. They are surrounded by mothers and babies to whom they had distributed souvenir coronation mugs – although by the expression on the children's faces, a bag of sweets would have been much more welcome! The cake they baked for the occasion was rumoured to have been so sensational that the Mayor and Mayoress had to fight their way towards it through the crowds.

The older generation wasn't forgotten at Chipping Norton, and a coronation tea party was arranged for them by the local fire brigade. They are shown waiting patiently for the tea to be served in the town's fire station. Both this and the previous picture were taken by the notable 'Chippy' photographer, Frank Packer.

In Cricket Road, Cowley, the children put on fancy dress before coming along to the street party which was part of their coronation celebrations. This time there was only one queen (of Hearts), a couple of cowboys and an Indian. The bus driver's attention is clearly wandering in a rather dangerous way.

The unusually wrapt expression on the faces of these children at Abingdon Terrace, Didcot, can be explained by the fact that their coronation street party was accompanied by a Punch and Judy show which was staged in a nearby field. The grown-ups present seem to be just as enthralled as the youngsters.

This photograph shows just a few of the large number of Didcot's senior citizens who were taken on the Old Folks' coronation outing to California, near Wokingham. It was taken when they were having tea in California and includes: (standing, left to right) Mr Moylan, the Revd W. Keating, the Mayor of Wokingham and Mrs Moylan.

These young competitors taking part in a fancy-dress contest were residents of the Vauxhall 'Camp' at Didcot, who had taken time off from their street party to be photographed. The Camp was the local name for Vauxhall Barracks, which still exists in the town.

Right: As part of their celebrations, the residents of Kingham decided to commemorate the coronation by constructing a new playground for the village's children. These youngsters are shown making the most of the slide on the day after the playground was opened.

Below: One senior citizen was the leading light at Kingham, where a coronation oak was planted to mark the occasion. Having laid aside his walking stick for a few minutes, Mr Bentley Burrows, the village's oldest resident, is pictured, spade in hand, about to finish the job.

In south Oxford, the residents of Donnington Road turned out in force to arrange a street party for their own youngsters. Apart from the usual party treats, this included a giant cake and some very unseasonable crackers.

At Radley another senior citizen was involved in the festivities when the coronation Queen, Sylvia Preou, was crowned by the village's oldest inhabitant, Mr Grimes. She is shown wearing a very convincing crown, complete with Victoria-style veil, and accompanied by her ladies-in-waiting.

At Thame the weather was very uncertain on Coronation Day, and at times it poured with rain. This is probably why these children are at an indoor party, unlike the great majority of celebrations in the county, which took place in the open air. The youngsters appear to be drinking out of their souvenir cups and using the saucers as plates.

Coronation celebrations went on for several days, and this street party, also held in Thame, took place on a sunny day the following week on the 'Rec', the Recreation Ground in Southern Road. (Author's collection)

The week after the coronation itself, it was the turn of the older generation of Thame to sit down to tea, also indoors. Strangely enough, apart from a few glasses or beer, there is no sign of any party food – although it might have already been eaten, and the tables cleared before this photo was taken.

As was usual, Wallingford marked the coronation by electing its own Queen. What was different, in this case, was her means of transport: this Austin was converted into a carriage fit for the Queen and her four attendants, and led an unusual motorcade of varied vehicles.

Also taken in Wallingford was this picture of competitors taking part in the town's coronation fancy-dress parade and contest. They are shown lined up for judging in the grounds of historic Wallingford Castle.

Up in Rosamund Road, Wolvercote, there was yet another street party. The unusual headgear, carrying the legend 'for the coronation', is being worn by adults and children alike.

3

FAIRS, FEASTS, CARNIVALS AND FESTIVALS

In September 1981, the weather for Wallingford fair was so bad that visitors got soaked. People joked that those who went on this ride – known as 'the Meteor' – had done so in order to get dried out: being a vertical centrifuge, it worked on the same principle as a spin-dryer. That year the Meteor was the only state-of-the-art ride at the fair, the rest of the attractions being traditional, such as the galloping horses and the big wheel. When the three-day fair was dismantled, the pools of muddy water left in the Kinecroft showed that the weather had once again lived up to its reputation for the event.

This photograph, which was taken in September 1906 from the junction of Broad Street and George Street, shows that the St Giles' fair of that year was packed with visitors. Particularly noticeable are the ladies in their Edwardian finery – including enormous summery hats. This part of the fair in Magdalen Street West is still largely made up of stalls offering all sorts of things to eat and drink, although nowadays butterscotch would cost considerably more than a penny, and the non-alcoholic sarsaparilla drink is seldom found outside health food shops.

Forty years on, in September 1946, this view of St Giles' fair shows few signs of wartime austerity, although this was only the second time that the fair had been held since the end of the Second World War. The whole of the street, from the church to the Martyrs' Memorial, is packed with people intent on enjoying themselves and spending money.

Taken in October 1955 at Woodstock fair, this photograph captures Mark Woolliscroft and Hilary Coleman enjoying a ride on a miniature galloping horse. The newspaper photographer notes that Mark had left his pram specially to ride on 'Gay' the galloper. Centred around the Town Hall, the ancient Charter Fair at Woodstock was crowded with stalls and amusements.

Back at St Giles' fair in 1965 when this picture was taken, boxing booths were very much a part of fairground life. The proprietor would work the crowd by offering £5 to anyone who could last three rounds with one of his champions – and although there were local hotheads and University Boxing Blues to take up the challenge, the prize was very rarely won. The large dogs, like this Dalmatian, which guarded the vans and stalls, added to the glamour.

Opposite above Some very different fair-goers were snapped in Abingdon in October 1956, including one wearing a dog-collar on the dodgems. This picture was taken during the afternoon, but the fare was 6d per person at any time and the 'One Way Round, NO bumping' rule strictly enforced, hence the name of the ride. Abingdon still has two fairs, the Michaelmas one (held in October and the longest street fair in Europe) and the Runaway Fair a week later.

Opposite below The expressions on the faces of these ladies on the Waltzer at Banbury fair in October 1961 sum up the excitement tinged with anxiety of the bigger fairground rides. This was part of the town's three-day Michaelmas fair and once again the question was asked as to whether it should be moved away from the town centre. Despite all the complaints about disruption, forty years on it is still held on its traditional site.

Nowadays the Helter Skelter marks the northern limit of St Giles', but in 1965 the stalls are shown extending beyond it and along the Woodstock and Banbury Roads. The large crowd of adults to the left of the entrance is made up of parents waiting to collect their children as they came hurtling down on the scratchy coconut mats.

Above: The fairground service took place in September 1967 on James Noyce's illuminated Gallopers at Witney Feast, held on the Leys. On the Monday of the two-day fair the weather was worse that it had been for many years, but even the mud underfoot didn't put off the visitors, who turned up in their hundreds.

Right: Among the entrants for the children's fancy dress at Charlbury Street Fair in October 1968 was three-year-old Stephen Fowler. On being declared the winner in the solo under-seven years' category for his 'Oh, brother!' costume, he burst into tears – just like being at the BAFTAs. The look on the face of his neighbour speaks volumes.

Members of this prize-winning group in the children's fancy-dress competition at Charlbury, also in October 1968, look much more cheerful. Dressed as 'Doddy's Little Diddy People', after comedian Ken Dodd's characters, they are Roland Asbridge (aged seven), John Porrill (eight), Caroline Sandford (six), Nigel Asbridge (ten) and Janice Porrill (six), all of whom came from Charlbury.

Ladies dressed in colourful medieval-style costumes were to be seen serving behind the stalls at the Charlbury Street 'Fayre' in October 1972. As usual, the second-hand bookstall drew the attention of many prospective buyers, while a blind eye was turned as children gambled away their pocket money as they tried to win sweets and toys by picking out playing cards.

At Cowley Feast in September 1960, no less a person than Alderman A.H. Kinchen, the Lord Mayor of Oxford, complete with chain of office, was sighted on the dodgems. In the true spirit of Town and Gown co-operation, his passenger was Mrs B.B. Lloyd, wife of the University's Senior Proctor, while Councillor W. Simpson drives the other car.

A prayer-meeting was held among the dodgems at Littlemore in August 1961. Hymns were played over the loudspeakers, and a congregation of about 100, most of them fair people, joined visiting evangelist Graham Spokes for a fairground service which lasted around forty-five minutes. Mr Spokes was very pleased with the attendance and planned to extend the services to include other fairs in the area.

Following the service, there was community singing, using the sides of the track as pews. Those attending are dressed in a mix of formal outfits suitable for church (including at least one hat) and more practical clothing for clambering on and off rides.

Village feasts do not always take the form of funfairs, although they may include a roundabout or two. The events usually include processions of floats and fancy-dress competitions, as shown by this entry at Harwell Feast in June 1962. The Flintstones – Fred and Wilma, Barney and Betty – were the stars of one of the most popular cartoons from the 1960s, although the pig's head didn't feature in the original cast.

Among the entrants for the fancy-dress competition at Harwell Feast in June 1962 were these children from Caldecott House. The Dr Barnardo's Home in Abingdon was opened in 1945 and played an important part in the lives of the town's young people until its closure in 1971. The beatnik outfit worn by the girl on the right of the picture would have been very topical in the early 1960s.

Above: Floats and participants in fancy dress make their way up the steep hill on a hot Saturday in July 1965, on their way to the Recreation Ground for the Burford Carnival. The procession was led by Carnival Queen Chantal Cartier, a hotel receptionist from France. This, the town's first carnival for twelve years, was very well attended, with attractions such as Bampton Morris men, a tug-of-war and a comedy football match.

Right: Pictured in May 1966 is Leonard Lovesey of Wardington, near Banbury, on a veteran tractor which was one of the attractions in the agricultural machinery section at that year's Oxfordshire Show. The tractor, a 1914 International Titan, owned by Saville (Tractors) Ltd of Banbury, was still in perfect running order. Until the firm bought it three years previously it had been working in Ireland.

Left: A record crowd of about 12,000 turned up for a veteran transport rally at Ward's Farm, Woodcote, near Reading, in July 1972. One of the stars was this 1870 Fowler plough engine. In this photograph, co-owner and steersman Bill Thame of East Hagbourne chats to crew member Jack Green. Rally entries ranged from penny-farthings and Rolls-Royces to steam rollers and old tractors.

Below: Boris the Fire-eater (or flame-thrower), of the Amazing Zolas, was one of the less conventional performers entertaining the crowds at Towersey Festival in August 1990. The festival, which was first held in 1964, now takes up a very long weekend and includes a folk and children's festival and a craft fair, and attracts star performers and visitors from all over the world.

Starting off in the 1970s, Fairport's Cropredy Convention has become one of the big dates in the folk music calendar every August, attracting up to 20,000 visitors over the three days that it is on. Organised by the bands themselves, it features artistes of the calibre of Status Quo, Rick Wakeman – and of course Fairport Convention. This photograph, taken in 1994, shows some of the vast crowd taking a rest between that year's acts, which included Lindisfarne and Roy Harper.

In June 1969, the Oxford Scouts' Carnival procession was led along the High Street by the 1st Shirley BP Guild Pipe Band. They are shown sweltering in their kilts, sporrans and plaids as they march past the bus stop at Queen's Lane.

At one time Abingdon carnival was quite a grand occasion, as shown by these photographs taken in May 1974. Despite a bitterly cold wind, hundreds of people turned out to watch about thirty floats come through the town centre. Here are Abingdon Sea Cadets in their boat, which was named after the long-serving battleship HMS *Matapan*.

Another float in the May 1974 Abingdon carnival parade belonged to the Jackie Bebbington School of Dancing. Miss Bebbington set up a dance school in 1950 and put on a pantomime every year for more than half a century. The girls on the float are all dressed as characters from Aladdin, apart from the 'wench' at the top left of the picture.

Abingdon Brownies and their float, complete with toadstool, at the 1974 carnival. The emblems on the side of the float represent the different patrols to which the girls belonged. Throughout the day, about forty-five Guides and Brownies showed a selection of arts and crafts at the Guide headquarters in Station Yard.

Medieval fashions from assorted eras were on display at Steeple Aston in September 1980. Thirty-five models paraded through the village and at nearby USAF Upper Heyford to advertise the Steeple Aston medieval fair. This included street stalls and a number of 'medieval' games, and was followed by a banquet with a menu of venison washed down with ale.

An arresting site at the Steeple Aston fair the same year: the Black Prince, shown here about to ride into battle. The scenario was that the Queen of Light and Beauty had been captured by a gang of wrestlers, and was to be held prisoner until the villagers handed over the ransom money. Among the attractions were a jousting machine, Morris and maypole dancing, hand-bell ringing, a mummers' play and a pig chase.

Guests posing for a knees-up picture at Burford Street Fair in June 1981. These Pearly families, from six London boroughs, had come along to add their cheerful patter to the locals', circulating with collecting tins among the crowds at the fair to raise money for cancer research. The fair, which also offered displays of sports cars and bikes and pottery and corn-dolly making, made more than £4,500 for the charity.

Another type of fair, and a very worthwhile one, is the charity fair. Oxfam, the Oxford Committee for Famine Relief, was established in the city and this photograph taken in August 1961 shows a 'summer fayre' organised entirely by children to help the charity. Admission was one penny and the same amount was charged to view pets and guess the name of a guinea pig, while most books and items of bric-à-brac cost a shilling.

Students have long been known for their ability to raise money and enjoy themselves at the same time, and Oxford undergraduates are no exception. The May Fair, shown here in May 1963, was organised by the Oxford University Freedom from Hunger Campaign Committee in the University Parks. Fishing in rather murky bathwater obviously had lots of appeal for these small boys, who are giving the game as much attention as their grandchildren would give to computer games.

The street market held at Blewbury in June 1985 was billed as a 'seventeenth-century' theme, with both Roundheads and Cavaliers encamped on the recreation ground for a skirmish performed on the Playclose by the English Civil War Society. Stalls, an ox roast and Morris dancing also featured. Pictured in costumes which were more Tudor than Stuart in appearance are Paul and Nicola Ellis and their daughter Chloe.

Above: In June 1985, Fritwell Carnival returned after a year's absence. Organised by the football club, most of the village's groups also took part, and the proceeds were shared between them. The carnival had taken place every year since the Silver Jubilee in 1977, except for 1984, when arrangements were left too late. In 1985 it started off with an egg-and-spoon race through the streets and went on to include a yard-of-ale contest. Members of the angling club are shown here on their circus-themed float.

Left: In 2001, it appeared that part of Sherwood Forest had moved from Nottinghamshire to Banbury in order to take part in the carnival there. The Foresters were in fact all workers from the Hella car accessory factory based in the town, and they won first prize for the best decorated float. Don Estelle, star of the television comedy *It Ain't Half Hot Mum*, serenaded the crowds in Spiceball Park, and also in attendance was a pipe and drum band from Hennef, Banbury's twin town in Germany.

Fun in the Parks, organised by the City Council, used to be a summer feature in Oxford. Various events similar to those found at street fairs and village fêtes were organised in the city's public parks. This photograph, taken in June 1990, shows 'sunflowers' from St Andrew's School in Headington taking part in the festivities in Hinksey Park. They were part of a parade which made its way along Cowley Road, High Street, St Aldates and the Abingdon Road.

Above: The people of Bampton are well known for their ability to organise all manner of crazy activities for raising money for charity. Taking part in the street fair held there in May 1992 was this busload of children, driven by Nigel the Clown under the watchful eye of Police Constable Steve Patrick.

Left: One of the traditional attractions at summer fêtes is the chance to lob a wet sponge at a prisoner in the stocks. In the pillory at the fun day, held at the Black Swan pub in Abingdon in May 1992, is Chris Pugh, who has just received a sponge in the mouth thrown from very close quarters.

Girls dressed in Victorian-style black stockings and white aprons danced around a maypole erected in the Upper High Street at Thame in June 1992. The maypole belonged to John Hampden School and the dancers were taking part in that year's Thame Street Fair.

These crowds are taking time out to relax whilst watching bands in South Park in Oxford as part of Caribbean Day. Steel bands have become a popular part of celebrations in the city thanks to its Afro-Caribbean community. Although this photograph was taken in July 1994, it has something of a 1970s feel.

And finally, a reminder that every successful event needs a good caterer: the caption to this photograph, taken in the Charlbury area, is 'At a garden fête, 1903 – Two hundred people on the spree, and only me to make the tea.' Pictured in charge of refreshments is local JP, baker and confectioner Mr G.J. Jones.

4

MAY DAY, MORRIS AND MUMMERS

The newly-elected Mayor of Ock Street, Stuart Jackson, is being chaired by fellow dancers on the Abingdon Traditional Morris Men's Mayor-Making Day in June 2001. The office of Mayor of Ock Street is unique to Abingdon and may have originated in a protest against the fact that so many townspeople were denied the right to vote for the Town Mayor proper. The Mayor of Ock Street holds office for a year and the electorate is made up of residents of the street, which is about a mile long.

This classic English village scene, taken in May 1985, includes all the necessary ingredients: an ancient church, a thatched cottage and children dancing round a maypole. The village is Charlton-on-Otmoor, where all thirty-four of its junior school children joined in the May Day celebrations. There was a parade from the school to St Mary's church, where a service was held before the dancing began. Charlton-on-Otmoor is well known for its May Day festivities, which have been photographed and documented since Victorian times.

Another place which has long been noted for its May Day activities is Iffley, just outside Oxford. Here, the boy and girl who were elected May King and Queen are passing under an arch of honour before making their way through the village streets accompanied by their attendants. May Kings are much rarer than Queens, probably because boys are less keen on dressing up for the part.

At Islip, another Otmoor village, maypole dancing by pupils from Dr South's School was part of the May Day celebrations in 1962. Preceded by a crown bearer, the May Queen Jane Steele led a procession of flower girls, and other festivities that year included country dances, singing games, and a mime play of 'Peter and the Wolf'. It ended with tea for the children in the village hall.

On May Day 1963, the May Queen of neighbouring villages Toot and Marsh Baldon was eleven-year-old Helen Greenaway, whose helpers took the opportunity of collecting for the People's Dispensary for Sick Animals. This was organised by Laura Middleton and by the May Queen's sister, Beryl, and raised £3 7s. The procession went round the Baldons singing May songs and leaving bunches of spring flowers at houses along the way.

A maypole was put up on the village green at Tackley for May Day 1966. The traditional setting, with its backdrop of stone cottages found in this part in this part of Oxfordshire, combined with a fiddler and the chaplet of flowers worn by some of the girl dancers, all gave the occasion a traditional feeling. The non-dancers appear to be providing stability for the maypole to make sure it doesn't topple onto those taking part.

This photograph was taken in the car park of the White House pub at Bladon on May Day 1986. The schoolchildren joined with the village playgroup to put on entertainments which featured all sorts of traditional characters – including the Lord and Queen of the May, Robin Hood and Maid Marion, as well as St George and the Dragon. As in past decades, the Garland and the Lady were paraded through the village.

On May Day at Begbroke in 1989, Royal Sun customers joined in with local children to dance round the maypole. Other attractions open to revellers were guessing the weight of a lively calf, throwing custard, rice pudding and water at the pub's barmaid, who was secured in the stocks, and the more customary crowning of the May Queen and fancy-dress competition.

These trumpeters, playing on the top of Magdalen Tower in 1981, are David White of Christ Church, Beverley Gray of The Queen's College, Michael Skitt of Witney and Andrew Butcher, also of Christ Church, all members of Oxford Silver Band. The fanfare and special lunch in the hall was to mark the completion of extensive repairs, which started in 1975 and finished in 1981, at a cost of more than £900,000.

Magdalen College choir pictured singing *Te Deum patrem colimus*, their seventeenth-century hymn to spring on the top of Magdalen Tower in 1986. They also sang an ode by John Fuller, set to music by Bernard Rose, both Fellows of the college.

This undated aerial photograph shows the huge May Morning crowds packing the lower end of Oxford's High Street as they come away from Magdalen Bridge, after listening to the choir singing their hymn to spring on the college tower at 6 a.m. Each year, the revellers surge back along the High Street to watch Morris dancers performing in various parts of the city, and to have breakfast in the pubs and cafés which open especially early to cater for them.

Morris men jiving outside Chipping Norton Town Hall in June 1961 proved that they knew all the latest dance routines. These members of Oxford City Morris Dancers were at Chipping Norton at the start of their tour of north Oxfordshire. The tour included Sibford Gower, where they joined forces with the village Folk Dancing Club for a party.

Headington can claim to have been the centre of a renaissance in Morris dancing, and William Kimber was its best-remembered expert. Here he is with young dancers from Margaret Road School in 1956. The boys had just been invited to perform at the Folk Dance Festival at the Albert Hall.

William Kimber was enough of a local celebrity to have a road named after him, a rare event for a living person. This photograph, dating from October 1958, shows dancers entertaining the crowd in the newly-named William Kimber Crescent. The music was provided by Mr Kimber himself (seated with the concertina).

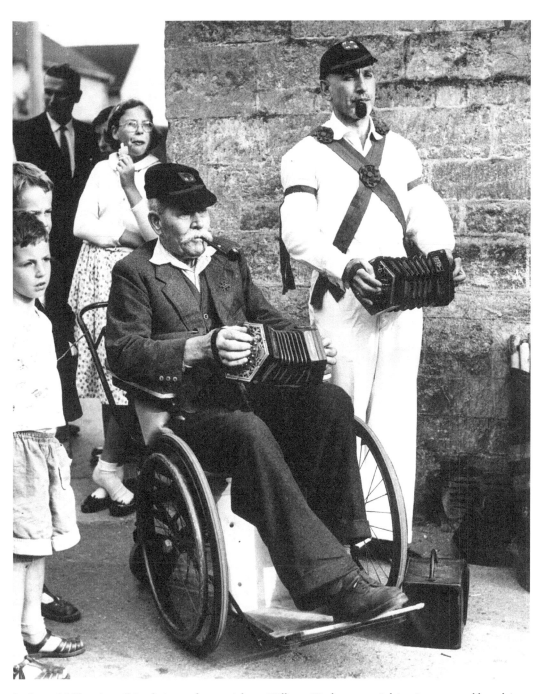

In June 1960, when this photograph was taken, William Kimber was eighty-nine years old and in a wheelchair. However, he was still a very skilful concertina player and is shown accompanying the Headington Quarry Morris Men. Unfortunately, Mr Kimber died a few months later, on Boxing Day of that year.

Above: In May 1964, the University Morris Men were just one of the dance troupes which performed at Kirtlington Lamb Ale. They are shown dancing in the playground of the village school during the feast. Although plenty of people are standing around as they dance, they are not taking much notice; Morris dancing is still looked on as nothing out of the ordinary in Oxfordshire today.

Left: Morris dancers in the garden of the White Horse pub in Ock Street, Abingdon, in September 1981: these are the Abingdon Traditional Morris Men, one of two Morris sides in the town. The music is provided by a fiddle and accordion, and the character in the foreground is the Fool with his bladder.

Les Argyle, aged fifty-seven, being chaired shoulder-high along Ock Street shortly after being elected Mayor of Ock Street in June 1984. Baker Les, Squire of Abingdon Traditional Morris Men, had been dancing for more than thirty years. The mayor-making ceremony, which dates from 1700, is one of the highlights of the Morris calendar and attracts sides from all over Britain.

Dancers from all over the country gathered in Oxford in September 1965 for the 100th meeting of the Morris Ring of England. Here are some of the 350 dancers who attended giving a display in the courtyard of the Golden Cross in Cornmarket.

Colonel Bill Morrell (right) proposes a toast to the old sign at the Red Lion, the oldest pub in Eynsham, in February 1986. The old and new landlords and their wives – Frank and Dorothea Harris, and Doug and Pam Walls – were present, and the Eynsham Morris Men danced in celebration at the reopening of the pub.

In Oxfordshire, Morris dancers start at an early age – as these youngsters showed in July 1989 when Chesterton Primary School Morris performed at King's Meadow Primary School in Bicester. Kitted out in bandoliers and bells and clutching handkerchiefs, the pupils, who unusually included several girls in their troupe, were led by their head teacher, Andy Reading.

May Day 1982 was marked by a schoolchildren's walk from Aston Rowant to Kingston Blount led by parents and the May Queen, Emma Clark (with her attendants, Clare Harwood and Nicola Longley). Music was provided by Brian Newton-Fisher (pictured), who dressed in a costume which was mixture of Morris and mummers. A combined event organised by the two communities was a fête held at the Shoulder of Mutton at Kingston Blount.

Morris dancing and mummers' plays are often performed by the same people, although the dancing is much more frequently seen. The plays, which portray the triumph of good over evil, are usually put on over the Christmas season, Boxing Day being the favourite time. There are many varieties of plays, although most show a marked similarity. Several of these characters, taking part in the annual Boxing Day fancy dress walk in Blewbury in December 1983, are from mumming plays and include St George and the Turkish Knight.

A centuries-old mummers' play was performed at four Blewbury public houses at Christmas 1967. Lead by Frank Geal of Harwell, the Blewbury Mummers followed a script taken from a collection published in 1888. It had taken Mr Geal four years to revive the play, helped by his brother Peter, Patrick Patterson, Johnny Walker, Fred Pargiter, Bruce Tofield and Tony Seaton.

Above: Bringing in the New Year in 1984 in their own unique way were the Wheatley Morris Men, who are shown doubling up as mummers at the Plough, Garsington as part of their tour of the pubs of Garsington and Wheatley. Although both their costumes and the text of the play have gradually altered over the years, the tradition has continued.

Left: Jack Finney, played by Mick Jones, is shown operating on the recently deceased Turkish Knight, better known as Chris Kingham. Both players belonged to Wheatley Mummers and they were performing in their own village, outside the White Hart In January 1981.

The age-old struggle between the forces of good and evil, as portrayed by Wheatley Mummers outside the Clifden Arms at Worminghall in November 1981. It proved too cold for them to stay outside for long, and so they went into the bar to perform their stick dance.

Long-standing Morris dancer, several-time Mayor of Ock Street and Keeper of the Scrapbook, Les Argyle was photographed as Father Christmas, dressed in paper strips while taking part in the Sunningwell mummers' play at Christmas 1985. The show was taken round nine pubs in Abingdon town centre, starting at the Crown in Ock Street and finishing up at the Broad Face in Bridge Street. With Les is 'the Doctor', played by Roger Cox.

5

SPORTS, GAMES AND OTHER AMUSEMENTS

This merry tortoise, chalked on the wall of Oriel Front Quad, demonstrates the importance of the river in Oxfordshire. He is celebrating Oriel's many victories in the Torpid 'bumps' races; these are similar to the famous Eights but are for less experienced rowers. The tortoise symbolises the college's rowers who make up the Tortoise Club. In one hand he holds a blade from the Oriel boat and in the other the Prince of Wales's feathers, adopted by the college as one of its badges as it was founded by Edward II, the first holder of the title. (Courtesy of Brian Archer)

Left: Although the University Boat Race takes place in London there is plenty of activity on the river at Oxford throughout the year. The leading event is the series of bump races which take place in the early summer. In this picture from the 1958 Eights, the Exeter College boat is about to catch Merton and register a bump, even though the two boats should not come into contact.

Below: All the college boats have names, most of them unusual and some rather fanciful. Here H.F. Mathews, a former Captain of Boats, is shown in 1960 christening a new Jesus College boat the *Nell Gwynne*; it is on the Isis, as the part of the Thames which flows through Oxford is called.

A Queen's College eight proudly shows off its new £2,350 boat in 1977, watched by the College Provost, Lord Blake. There had been some doubt as to whether they would be allowed on the river at all, due to its being swollen, but permission was given for a short row up to Folly Bridge and back.

In 1980, students at Oriel College were forbidden to jump through the flames as part of the traditional boat-burning ceremony which took place when a college became Head of the River after Torpids. This was because a girl had been burnt while doing so. This photograph was taken at a previous ceremony. Nowadays an old boat is ceremonially hacked to pieces as the present ones are made of fibreglass and are very expensive.

Successful college eights will go on to compete in national and international events outside Oxford and even abroad. Here the Keble First Eight of 1961, smartly turned out in traditional boating gear, are off to Reading to compete in the Regatta there.

In 1986, the Tiddington tug o'war team representing Oxfordshire managed to bring the number of wins to seventeen-all against the neighbouring village of Ickford in Buckinghamshire. The contest for the Coronation Cup is held across the River Thame at Ickford Bridges. That year, members of the winning team were presented with the traditional bottle of whisky donated by Richard Chandler of Church Farm, Ickford.

POOH-STICK COMPETITION RULES

THE REFEREE'S DECISION IS FINAL.

POOH STICKS MUST BE DROPPED NOT THROWN.....

ANY PERSON WHO DROP'S THEIR POOH STICK BEFORE......
REFEREE'S SIGNAL WILL BE DISQUALIFIED.....

No PERSON SHALL ATEMPT TO NOBBLE OR HINDER COMPETITOR

ANY HINT OF BIG SYNDICATE BETTING COUP WILL CAUSE
COMPITITION TO BE DECLARED NULL AND VOID.....

ANY PERSON SUBSTITUTING OFFICIAL POOH STICKS WILL BE
PUNISHED AND BANNED FOR LIFE......

IT IS AN OFFENCE TO OFFER BRIBES TO REFEREE
OR ANY OFFICIAL

ANY COMPETITOR USING DRUGS OR STIMULANTS WILL BE
DISQUALIFIED

THE PLYING OF GIN OR ANY STRONG ALCOHOLIC BEVERAGE
TO REFEREE IS TO BE DISCOURAGED

BEING DRUNK IN CHARGE OF A POOH-STICK IS A OFFENCE

Fans of Winnie-the-Pooh will remember that the bear and his friends used to stand on a bridge and drop sticks into the river then rush across to the other side to see whose stick came out first. A keen Royal National Lifeboat Institute supporter, Lynn David, lock-keeper at Day's Lock, Long Wittenham, hit upon the idea of using the game to raise funds for the charity. It became an annual event, attracting entrants from all over Britain and beyond. Here are the Open Pooh-Stick Championships rules as displayed in 1985, when there were 120 competitors.

Left: The Pooh-Stick Champion in 1984 was twelve-year-old Chloe Wilson, who lived nearby at Little Wittenham. She is shown with the large bear which was her prize; Chloe told the press, 'There's a faster current in the middle so I just got into the middle position and stayed there.'

Below: Crowds gathered around the RNLI banner in 1991. When Mr David retired some ten years after the start of the Championships, responsibility for arranging the event passed to the local Rotary Club of Sinodun. It continues to be featured in the national, and occasionally international, news broadcasts.

In the days before school outings included skiing holidays and visits to other continents in the name of education, one of life's highlights was a river trip on a steamer. Salters have been leaders in this field for more than a century. These Oxford youngsters, armed with macs and packed lunches, can't wait to board a steamer at Folly Bridge in March 1968.

The first mention of a college tortoise was at Trinity College in George III's reign and the earliest photograph of them, which dates from 1898, was taken at Corpus Christi College. Today the Tortoise Fair, which includes racing reptiles, takes place at Corpus in May and has been described as 'unique to Oxford and undoubtedly the best tradition ever.' Here Fred is being presented with the South Oxford Champion's Certificate by Dr David Charles-Edwards of Corpus Christi.

Aunt Sally is a pub game where players throw batons at a wooden skittle known as a doll. Until recently it was seldom found outside Oxfordshire, where it is very popular, but it is now more widespread and several universities have teams. The captain of Exeter College team, Colin Harrison, was photographed in action in 1960 at The Old Gate House (now the White House), in Botley Road.

The Aunt Sally team from the Paradise House (now the Castle Tavern) in Paradise Street are seen sorting out their results cards before a home match against the George at Stanton St John in 1963. They are, from left to right: D. Stowell, the captain, B. Fouracre, P. Mead, R. Nixon, J. Staine, D. Sullivan, N. Brown and E. Worland.

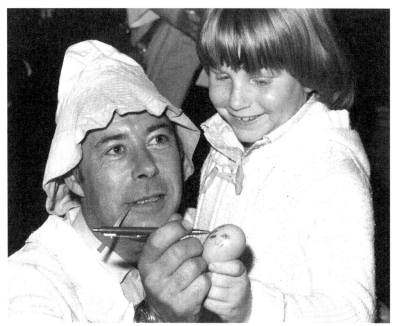

Jarping (otherwise known as egg-dumping) is normally confined to the North of England. However, shown jarping at Chinnor in April 1981 are seven-year-old Samantha Slough, who holds her egg, and Chief Jarp Master PC Mick Field, who marks up another conquest on the shell. The World Egg Jarping championship takes place annually at Peterlee in County Durham.

Another egg-related Easter-time competition is egg rolling at Blewbury, shown here in April 1982. That year the event was started by the Vicar of Blewbury, the Revd Hugh Pickles, whose technique was to nudge his entry down the slope using his nose. It is held in the Chalk Pit, and although the eggs are of course hard-boiled, there are still plenty of casualties. One of the prizes is for the best-dressed egg and former entrants have worn skis, tutus and wellington boots.

In June 1962, the second barrel-rolling race was held at Kidlington. Barrels were rolled from the King's Arms, Kidlington to the King's Arms, Gosford. The winners, for the second time running, were the Old Southfieldians Rugby Club, who won a 'niner' barrel of beer and the coveted barrel-shaped trophy. Pictured here are some of the 'tramps' who took part in the event.

Part of Rycotewood College's Rag Week in Thame in May 1986 was this tractor haul from Thame to Chinnor and back. The students hoped to raise over £2,000 to help the town hospital's extension appeal, the Scouts' new headquarters fund, the old peoples' Christmas party and the Thames Valley Police benevolent fund.

Together with their partners, the Mayors of Witney, Woodstock, Chipping Norton, Burford and Carterton dressed up in Edwardian costume for their annual croquet match at Woodstock in September 1987. Here Derrick Burfitt, chair of West Oxfordshire Sports Advisory Council, supervises the winning shot played by Mrs Jane Blake of Woodstock. The rules of the game were formalised at Chastleton House, to the north of the county.

Four carloads of car-workers from Cowley came over for a gurning contest at the Red Lion, Wardington in December 1983. One of them, Philip 'Bomber' Harris, was the winner, and was presented with an inscribed lavatory seat. The event is more common in the North of England, where the World Championships take place each year at Egremont in Cumbria.

This photograph, taken in June 1955, shows competitors lining up for the Whitsuntide Great Shirt Race which takes place each year at Bampton: runners have to push a partner in a pram-type vehicle along a course of about half a mile, stopping off at the town's pubs and drinking six half-pints along the way.

In June 1968, the rules of the Great Shirt Race were tightened up and a warning given that all of the beer in the half-pint glasses positioned on a table outside each of the town's eight pubs had to be downed. 'All must be deposited inside, not outside. Big Brother will be watching you at each pub to check that there is no flagrant whatsname of the regulations.' The twenty-nine pairs raced from one end of Bampton to the other and then back to the Square. The prize, a nine-gallon barrel of beer, was won by Jimmy Townsend and Frank Hudson, representing the Eagle.

Les Faulkner, the eighty-four-year-old Sheikh of Blewbury, took part in the village's eleventh annual Boxing Day Walk in 1981 when more than £220 in coppers was raised for the local playground appeal. The aim was to collect enough coins to lift Les's 9½ stone weight off the ground. The walk started off at the Load of Mischief, moved on to the Blewbury Inn and finished off at the Red Lion, with participants forcing down pints along the way.

Above: This mock hunt on hobby-horses, which was held at Bampton in December 1990, was well in advance of the ban on fox-hunting. The huntsmen are pictured on their hobby-horses outside the Jubilee Inn posing for a group photograph with 'the Fox', Paul MacGrath, at the start of their fund-raising events.

Left: This penny-farthing rider making his way to the annual Harwell Feast in June 1962 is Mr G. Grant of Drayton, near Abingdon. He is riding his 1874 model. That year the feast attracted some 3,000 holiday-makers. One of the events was a 7 mile road race through Rowstock, Chilton, Hagbourne Hill, Upton Bridge and Folly Hill.

This late-Victorian photograph shows visitors enjoying a trip out to Uffington Castle, near the famous White Horse ancient chalk figure on a Bank Holiday in the 1890s. A fair was held there with stall, games, competitions and refreshments, and this was revived as part of the 2000 Millennium celebrations.

Less energetic visitors gently picnicking and enjoying the spectacular views from White Horse Hill, near to the Horse itself, in July 1958; however, they had negotiated a hard climb by car and on foot to reach this spot.

Dancing has always been one of the best ways for boy to meet girl and these young ladies are all dressed up in their finery for a New Year dance in 1962. The expression on their anxious faces shows what an ordeal it was to have no option but to sit around the edge of the dancefloor watching and waiting for a boy to come over and ask them to dance.

Fashion shows were a very popular way of advertising what a shop had to offer and raising money for charity at the same time. In this photograph, taken in September 1960 at an autumn fashion show organised by the Co-op in Banbury, it is hard to believe that the young girl dressed in such a matronly coat is still in her teens.

Above: The world record for the longest hand-rolled cigarette was claimed in Oxford in 1971. It stretched for 50ft along Broad Street, where it is shown outside the Clarendon Building. The constructors were sponsored and the money raised was donated to cancer research. The cigarette, which cost about £10 and took 2 hours, 40 minutes to make, was found to be unsmokeable and was afterwards destroyed.

Left: Traffic cones placed on the heads of the statues of various University worthies are not unusual in Oxford. This one, which formed the hat of a statue in a niche on the High Street frontage of Oriel College's Rhodes Building in 1978, was way above the heads of passers-by. The wearer was Cardinal Allen, a sixteenth-century member of Oriel.

Before the middle of the twentieth century, when they fell out of favour, hoaxes were very much a part of Oxford student life. One of the most successful was the Ibsen Jubilee Exhibition of 1956, which fooled over 100 visitors and even newspaper reporters. Organised by members of the (then) St Catherine's Society, who even printed a catalogue, the exhibition was reviewed by the *Oxford Mail* before eventually being exposed by a senior member of the paper's staff.

Adjoining colleges Balliol and Trinity acquired the reputation of being bad neighbours, to the extent of playing rather unpleasant practical jokes on each other. One example of these so-called jokes was the laying of a turf carpet in Trinity Junior Common Room, carried out by these members of Balliol in 1963. They were told to remove it – or else!

These five chamber pots making a graceful addition to the Trinity College skyline, where they were placed on pinnacles in 1954, were described in the press as 'household utensils'. Chamber pots were sometimes fixed in position with cement and had to be smashed by firing at them with rifles.

These three bikes were just a few of a number of bicycles which appeared among the pinnacles and chimneys of Brasenose College in 1958. It was suggested that they were brought into the college and hauled up from the quadrangle and then over the roof. One of the bikes visible from the High Street was adorned with a chamber pot.

A hand-painted fake zebra crossing appeared in the High Street near University College at 2 o'clock one morning in 1980. It was the work of the college Rugby Club and was realistic enough to take in at least one pedestrian who used it to cross the road. Removing the plasticised emulsion paint cost the City Engineer's Department £90, and one of the perpetrators was charged with criminal damage while attempts were underway to find the others.

6

THE OXFORDSHIRE YEAR

Throughout the year, Oxfordshire parishes celebrate the feast days of their patron saints. In this photograph, taken in 1961, Yarnton church choir is shown processing through the village as part of the celebrations for the parish's patron saint on 24 August, St Bartholomew's Day. A piano on a trailer provided the music for the procession which was held in aid of the church restoration fund, for which £3,000 was needed. Several stops were made along the way for hymns and prayers. It ended with Evensong.

A Plough Monday party was given by the Mayor of Woodstock, Councillor Dr Alistair Robb-Smith, and members of the Borough Council in January 1967. Plough Monday is the first Monday after Epiphany (or Twelfth Night), and marks the return to work at the end of the Christmas period. The name derives from the starting of ploughing after the holiday.

Wallingford is one of several places in the county which organise pancake racing on or around Shrove Tuesday to mark the beginning of Lent. Nick Grierson (in the foreground, wearing glasses), an employee of the town's branch of Barclay's Bank, was photographed taking part in the 1990 race, although the people in the crowd don't give him a second glance as they put money into the collector's bucket.

These strangely-clothed characters were getting in some practice for the 1990 annual Shrove Tuesday pancake race at Drayton near Abingdon. Pictured are members of the John Mason School team: Sarah Davis, Gillian Parrott, Marsha Locke, Laura Wolley, Emma Dix and Zoe Loran. The race was won by the table-tennis club team, who were dressed as burglars.

The Oxford Welsh Glee Club, under conductor John Bettershell, shown here performing in April 1975, was formed in 1928 by a group of young Welsh singers who had recently arrived in Oxford from South Wales to work in the car industry at Cowley. The club sung in venues as varied as Oxford Prison and charity events – and, of course, to celebrate on or around 1st March, St David's Day, every year.

Here are about twenty energetic participants setting off on the Radley annual Good Friday Walk in 1987. The first walk took place in 1963, with the route from the Bowyer Arms into Oxford and back, a round trip of about 12.5 miles. Nowadays there is the option of shorter walks such as the Half Walk and the Triangle Walk round Lower Radley.

One of the highlights of Easter was the beautifully decorated chocolate eggs which were produced by Oxfordshire's bakers and confectioners such as George E. Weeks and Co. Ltd at their Swan Bakery in St Ebbes. In this picture, Mr E.W. Tarrant and Miss Joyce Hern are shown decorating some of the thousands of Easter eggs which Weeks produced in 1962.

Oxford has a sizeable Irish community and its own Miss A. Flood School of Irish Dancing, members of which are shown in 1971 performing at the Eire Og (Oxford) Hurling and Football Club's seven-a-side tournament on Easter Monday at the Iffley Road Rugby Ground.

The winner of the second prize at Kidlington Evergreen Club's Easter bonnet contest in April 1973 was Mrs Ceridwen Davies; this was hardly surprising, as she had trained as a milliner. Mrs Davies's entry, which was piled high with fluffy chicks, was modelled by her helpful husband Albert. The first prize went to Mr and Mrs Reginald Fisher, who are standing behind Mr and Mrs Davies.

Above: Wing Commander R.L. Lamb of RAF Brize Norton takes the salute at the St George's Day parade in Witney in 1972. The procession is shown marching past District Commissioner D.J. Cashman and Chairman of Witney, Urban District Council, H. Kitto. The Cub Scouts are making their way back along Church Green and St Mary's church is in the background.

Left: At Whitsun 1952, 1,100 children and 300 adults from all over the diocese gathered in Christ Church Cathedral to donate their gift of Whitsun farthings to the Oxford Diocesan Fund. The Bishop of Oxford, Dr K.E. Kirk, is shown receiving them. The total amount of money given was estimated to be in excess of the £1,314 13s 10½d (made up of 1,262,105 farthings) contributed the previous year.

Children from parishes in Oxfordshire, Buckinghamshire and Berkshire talking to the Bishop of Oxford, Dr Harry Carpenter, after the Whitsun gifts service in 1961. The money collected went towards building new churches, repairing old ones, and helping deaf and dumb children and others in hospital.

Candidates and their friends celebrating with the customary champagne, or, as is more usual, bottles of sparkling wine, after the Final Exams in June 1966. Traditionally, this took place outside the Examination Schools in the High Street, which constituted something of a health and safety hazard. Nowadays, however, the University authorities are much stricter and festivities are confined to college premises.

At Oxford University, degrees are conferred at a number of ceremonies throughout the year, not just after the examination results are announced. Graduands apply to come to the ceremony of their choice and so there is a good blend of degrees conferred at each, from the higher doctorates to the Bachelors. In this picture, new BAs wait to be joined by their admiring friends and families. (Author's collection)

The weather for the Encaenia (the annual conferral of honorary degrees) is known for being fine, but this was not the case in June 1968. Umbrellas were the order of the day as senior members of the University and that year's honorands did their best to protect their expensive academic dress from the rain. The procession is shown lining up in Oriel College's Front Quad prior to leaving for the Sheldonian Theatre where the ceremony is held.

The outdoor pulpit at Magdalen College decorated ready for the annual open-air sermon around 1950. It lapsed between 1766 and 1896, when it was revived by the future Archbishop of Canterbury, Cosmo Lang, who was at that time a member of the college. Nowadays the sermon is preached on the Sunday falling nearest to 24 June, St John the Baptist's day. Outdoor sermons were not unusual and were organised for raising money – and at the same time, to make sure that the *hoi polloi* had no excuse to go inside the building hosting the event.

Mr and Mrs E.A.C. Parker of the Bear and Ragged Staff at Cumnor were photographed in October 1961 busy arranging the harvest fare which the pub's customers had collected and which would later be raffled off for charity or distributed to needy villagers.

Opposite: Ten-year-old Jayne Strickland puts the final touches to a scarecrow and Martin Bird, also aged ten, adds a cabbage to the display at the Harvest Festival at St Christopher's School, Cowley in October 1966. The service, attended by the Vicar of Cowley the Reverend Parry Okeden, formed part of the school's morning assembly. The produce was later distributed among elderly residents of the parish.

This long queue is made up of schoolchildren waiting to bring their harvest festival offerings into Ambrosden church in October 1968. The fresh fruit, flowers and vegetables from their parents' gardens and allotments are very different from the tinned and pre-packed produce available for children to bring nowadays.

Bampton is well known locally for being a leading producer of giant pumpkins, some of which are so bulky that they have to be brought to the weigh-in at the village hall by trolley and wheelbarrow. In October 1999 the winner was John Buckingham, who was presented with a silver cup by Bampton May Queen, Laura Radband.

These toddlers at the Guy Fawkes' Night celebrations at the Slade Hospital in 1966 seem to be torn between enjoyment and fear of the sparklers which they are holding. Of course, nowadays this hands-on approach would be strictly banned due to health and safety restrictions.

Above: Bonfire (or Guy Fawkes') Night has been a feature of the English autumn for hundreds of years and Oriel College has records of a public bonfire costing 7s being held in its Front Quad in the seventeenth century. These pupils at Banbury Primary School are putting together their guy on 5 November 1971. The reason that his hands and feet are so enormous is that, when complete, the guy would be all of 10ft tall.

Left: These eight enterprising pupils from the Manor School in Didcot used a wheelchair to bring their own realistic guy along to the town's Round Table firework display in 1993.

Town Mayor Mr George Boyd was given the task of judging the Best Guy Competition at Bicester in November 1982. In all, forty-four guys, pushed along in wheelbarrows, prams and pushchairs, turned out on parade in a procession which was led through the town by the Air Training Corps. The winners, Thomas and Victoria Hollis, were given a £5 book token and their guy given pride of place on top of the Longfields bonfire.

Local Cubs were out in force at this public carol singing in 1965. Although they look as if they were out in the countryside, the singers were in fact in Oxford city centre, standing on the walled-off area in front of St John's College in St Giles. The tree belongs to the college.

Lots of young villagers gathered together to sing carols at a farm in the village of Sunningwell in December 1963. Sitting out in the cold on these scratchy straw bales must have felt very seasonal and the nearest thing to being in the original Christmas stable.

Helped by Mrs Joy Langton, sixty pupils from the infants' section at William Fletcher School, Yarnton, sent their own letters and pictures to Father Christmas in December 1973. The children were delighted to receive a special card each in return, courtesy of the Post Office, with a message from Santa inside.

There was no need to write to this Santa, as he appeared in person at a shop in Banbury in 1969. Despite the dubious beard – and even though there was no magic grotto, elves or fairies – the look on this little girl's face captures the true enchantment of Christmas.

Mr F. Berry, Mr W. Frances and Mr W. Green, employees at Oliver and Gurden's, who helped make the 6,132 Christmas puddings which the company produced in 1966. In total, these weighed 9 tons, cost £2,500 and were exported to Paris for distribution across France. They had been made to a secret recipe owned by Keble College, similar to traditional ones, but not available in the shops. Travelling in the same consignment as the puddings were forty-two Christmas cakes, a sample of English festive food for French food importers to enjoy.

In December 1978 Yarnton School was in the news again when an alternative Nativity play was put on by its pupils. This play, in which all the school's ninety-three children took part, differed from the conventional version in that it was set in the American West and the characters were cowboys and Indians.

Children from Nazareth House Home signed a Christmas card which was to be sent to the Oxford Covered Market's very own Father Christmas in December 1965. The notice apologises for his absence. For the rest of the year he was the well-known Oxford character Jimmy Dingle, who raised money for local charities, in particular the Radcliffe Infirmary. Wearing the Viking horned helmet is John Reed, who organised the collection of toys.

The village pantomime is one of the highlights of the year and very much a communal activity. Steeple Aston's production in 1979 was *Cinderella*, written and directed by the rector, Canon Michael Hayter, and organised through the village-hall committee to raise funds for improving the building. Pictured, from the left, are Peter Roberts as Buttons, Claire McKinley as Cinderella and Ron Roberts as Baron Hardup.

Opposite: When these Fire Brigade Santas appeared on the streets of Oxford in December 1963, it was in order to get over a serious message by handing out leaflets on fire safety to shoppers in Cornmarket Street. This was part of a campaign backed up by a fire engine decorated with safety posters. At that time Christmas decorations were a real fire hazard, the most dangerous of which were lighted candles on the tree.

Other titles published by The History Press

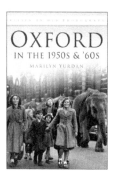

Oxford in the 1950s & '60s

MARILYN YURDAN

Oxford in the 1950s & '60s offers a rare glimpse of life in the city during this fascinating period. As this amazing collection of 200 photographs shows, there is much more to these two decades than pop groups and mini skirts. Including views of Oxford's streets and buildings, shops and businesses, pubs and hotels, the Colleges and University departments, as well as some of the villages which form the suburbs of the city, this book is sure to appeal to all who remember these decades and everyone who knows and loves Oxford.

978 0 7524 5219 7

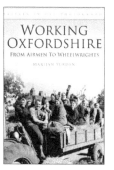

Working Oxfordshire: From Airmen to Wheelwrights

MARILYN YURDAN

Featured in this book are carvers and barrel makers, university employees and leather-workers, hop-pickers and bee-keepers, brewers and marmalade makers, railwaymen and bus drivers, thatchers and blacksmiths, and, of course, shops aplenty, including an ironmonger's which dates back to Tudor days. With 200 superb photographs this book will appeal to everyone with an interest in the history of the county, and also awaken memories of a bygone time for those who worked, shopped or simply remember these Oxfordshire firms, trades and businesses.

978 0 7524 5585 3

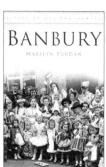

Banbury In Old Photographs

MARILYN YURDAN

This superb selection of 200 photographs provides a nostalgic insight into the changing history of Banbury over the last century. Each image is accompanied by a detailed caption, bringing the past to life and describing many aspects of life in the town, including chapters on work, industry, schools, markets and local events – including the annual carnival, College Rag, and funfair – and providing a vital record of vanished vistas and past practices.

978 0 7524 5606 5

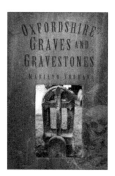

Oxfordshire Graves and Gravestones

MARILYN YURDAN

Local author Marilyn Yurdan takes the reader on a tour of the county's graveyards, including the largest Anglo-Saxon cemetery in England and a Medieval Jewish cemetery under Oxford Botanic Garden, and reveals the poignant, humorous, and sometimes gruesome history behind Oxfordshire's graves and gravestones. Among the gravestones featured here are those commemorating politicians, academics, soldiers, artists, poets and writers, as well as some more unusual people, including the first English balloonist, the soldier who fired the first shot at Waterloo, and a Maori lady.

978 0 7524 5275 9

Visit our website and discover thousands of other History Press books.
www.thehistorypress.co.uk